African Cu

50 Excellent African Recipes

BY

Julia Chiles

Copyright 2019 - Julia Chiles

OOOOOOOOOOOOOOOOOOOOOOOOOOOOOOOOOOOO

License Notes

No part of this Book can be reproduced in any form or by any means including print, electronic, scanning or photocopying unless prior permission is granted by the author.

All ideas, suggestions and guidelines mentioned here are written for informative purposes. While the author has taken every possible step to ensure accuracy, all readers are advised to follow information at their own risk. The author cannot be held responsible for personal and/or commercial damages in case of misinterpreting and misunderstanding any part of this Book

OOOOOOOOOOOOOOOOOOOOOOOOOOOOOOOO

Table of Contents

Introduction 7

Beef Bobotie 8

Doro Wat 12

Sadza 15

Chermoula 17

Tanzanian Inspired Vegetarian Pilau Rice 19

Magwinya 21

Biltong 23

West African Inspired Peanut Soup 26

Kefta Briouat 29

Moroccan Inspired Tagine 32

No Tagine Chicken Tagine 35

Okra Pressure Cooker Tagine 38

Chicken Durban Curry 41

Sambal (honey glazed Moroccan Carrots) 44

Lamb Tagine a.k.a Mrouzia Traditional Version 46

Tagine Cooker Mrouzia 49

Quick Easy Ras El Hanout Spice Mix 52

Chickpea Tagine with Carrots 55

Khobz dyal Smida -Moroccan Semolina Bread 58

Khobz- Moroccan White Bread 61

Easy Vegetable Ragu Over Couscous 63

Tfaya 66

Onion Mezgueldi 69

Mezgueldi M'chermel 71

Pressure Cooker Stewed Lentils 73

Easy African Stove Top Lentils and Okra 76

Easy Ground Beef Lentil Veggie Stew 79

Harira 82

20 Minute Pressure Cooker Harira 85

Lamb Harira Over Yellow Couscous 88

Kalinti 91

Easy Harissa Spice Mix 94

Stew Beef Merguez 97

Ground Beef Merguez Stew 99

Easy Homemade Merguez Spice Mixture 101

Zesty Chicken with Fried Almonds 103

Moroccan Inspired Vegetable Soup 106

African Inspired Sweet Potato Chicken Soup 109

Moroccan Beef Stew 112

Moroccan Inspired Beef Stew for the Crock Pot 115

African Inspired Pork Carnita Meat 118

Crockpot Tandoori Pork Carnita Meat 121

Savory Spicy Beef 124

Crockpot Taquitos 127

Moroccan Crockpot Burritos 131

Moroccan Chicken Pizza.. 134

46 One Pot Chicken Harissa.. 137

Harissa Inspired Chicken Lettuce Wraps..................... 140

Crockpot Shredded Harissa Meat................................ 142

Harissa Fried Shrimp.. 145

Harissa Inspired Beef Ribs... 148

Author's Afterthoughts.. 150

About the Author 151

Introduction

Do you believe the ingredients determine how the dish is cooked? If so, the impetus behind African cooking is the perfect methodology for you! Hearty stews; root vegetables; savory herbs, spices and seasonings; plus, so much more for the discerning appreciative palette!

Beef Bobotie

South Africa's national dish!

Makes: 2 serving.

Ingredients:

- 1 tablespoon butter
- 2 onions, diced or grated
- 2-2 ½ tsp garlic, minced or grated
- 1 1/2 teaspoon ginger, minced or grated
- 1 3/4 teaspoon curry powder
- 4 cloves
- 4 tablespoons chutney (we used Mrs. Balls)
- 1- 1 1/2 lbs. ground beef
- 1 2/3 tablespoon vinegar
- 1/3 tablespoon Worcestershire sauce
- 1 beef low sodium broth cube or 1 tsp bullion broth paste (ex. Better Than Bullion)
- 4 slices white bread (crusts removed soaked in milk)
- 2 egg
- 1 cup milk
- 1 ¼ teaspoon turmeric
- 1 tablespoon double cream, optional
- Salt Pepper to taste
- 3-5 bay leaves

Directions:

Preheat oven to 350.

In pot warmed over medium high heat, sauté butter, onion, ginger, garlic 2-3 minutes.

Stir in and sauté curry powder, cloves, ground beef, vinegar, Worcestershire sauce, vinegar, broth/paste. Sauté approx. 5 minutes or until all ground beef is brown.

Add in soaked bread pieces.

Transfer mixture into casserole dish, cover, and bake 38-45 minutes.

In the meantime, whisk together eggs, milk, and turmeric and for thickness add in cream.

Season with salt and pepper.

Pour over hamburger mixture when done.

Top with bay leaves and bake another 15-20 minutes.

Usually served with spicy yellow rice and chutney but any strong, fragrant rice will do.

This dish is best over spicy yellow rice but can be substituted with potatoes or pasta. You can also add sweet items such as raisins as a natural sweetener. The goal with this dish is not just to strike a balance between spicy and sweet, but to never let the sweetness be overshadowed by the spicy flavors!

Doro Wat

Also known as tsebhi dorho.

Makes: 4-5 servings.

Ingredients:

- 2-3 lbs. thighs and drumsticks
- 2-3 tablespoons lemon
- 3-4 tablespoons vegetable oil or niter kibbeh (fragrant butter)
- 3-5 teaspoons berbere spice mix
- 3-4 red onions
- 2 ½ -3 tablespoons garlic, grated or minced
- ½ tablespoon ginger, minced
- salt pepper to taste
- 1 ½ cups water or chicken stock (more if needed)
- 3/4 tablespoon garam masala
- 7-8 eggs

Directions:

1-2 hours before cooking, marinate chicken in lemon juice.

For speedy version of Doro Wat, blend onions, garlic, and ginger into a paste.

For authentic Doro Wat, let onions sweat in a Dutch Oven till they reduce and then form into a paste.

Bring pot or skillet to low heat high heat and add chicken pieces 5-6 minutes, turning halfway thru.

Sprinkle with Garam masala and add water if needed.

Meanwhile, start boiling the eggs.

Transfer to serving plates topping each with whole, shelled eggs or slices.

Sadza

An African staple that's also known as ugali, nshima, pap and phaleche. Accompanies a flavorfull fish or meat prepared for dinner or lunch; thus, it purposely lacks flavor to allow the protein to shine.

Makes: 4 servings.

Ingredients:

- 6-7 scoops of mealie-meal
- ¾ - 1 cup cold water
- 3-4 cups boiling water

Directions:

In pot mix mealie-meal with cold water.

Meanwhile, in another pot, bring 3-4 cups of water to a boil.

Mix both pots together then bring to a boil, cover, reduce heat to low and simmer 20 minutes.

Add mealie-meal ½ tsp at a time and stir well, repeating until desired consistency is reached.

If desired, again cover and simmer 5 minutes.

Chermoula

A Moroccan spice paste used for adding depth and dimension to proteins!

Makes: 2-4 cups worth.

Ingredients:

- 1 large bunch cilantro, chopped
- 2-3 tablespoons garlic, minced
- 1 tablespoon paprika
- 1 1/4 tablespoon cumin
- 2/3 – ¾ teaspoon salt
- 1 1/2 teaspoon ginger, thinly sliced or minced
- 2/3 teaspoon cayenne pepper
- 1/2 teaspoon saffron threads
- 3 tablespoons vegetable oil
- ½ tablespoon lemon juice

Directions:

In a large glass bowl mix together cilantro, minced garlic, paprika, cumin, salt,

ginger, cayenne pepper, saffron threads, oil, lemon juice.

Use to marinate fish, beef, veggies, or anything else you can think of!

Tanzanian Inspired Vegetarian Pilau Rice

Often emulated, pilau's use of spices change by region and can include such delicacies as toasted legumes!

Makes: 4 servings.

Ingredients:

- 1 tablespoon butter or ghee
- 1 onion, diced
- ½ tablespoon garlic
- 4-6 cardamom pods
- ½ -1 tablespoon cinnamon
- 2/3 teaspoon ground cumin
- 1/3 teaspoon of black pepper
- 2/3 teaspoon ground cloves
- 2 1/2 cups of Basmati rice
- 1 1/2 cup of coconut milk
- 3 cups of vegetable stock or boiling water

Directions:

In heavy pot or Dutch oven, melt butter or ghee and sauté onions 3-4 minutes.

Stir in rice and add all dry ingredients (garlic, cardamom, cumin, pepper cloves.

Stir in coconut milk and stock then bring to boil, cover, reduce heat, simmer 20 minutes.

Magwinya

A doughnut type of bread, it is much favored and sought after.

Makes:

Ingredients:

- 5 cups flour
- 5 tablespoons sugar
- 3 teaspoons instant yeast
- 1 teaspoon salt
- 1-2 tablespoon vegetable oil
- 2 cups warm water

Directions:

In large bowl, combine flour, sugar, instant yeast, salt, oil, water.

Cover with a towel and put in a cool, dry locale for 1 hour.

Will double in size, knead again 4-5 minutes then let sit 10 minutes.

Bring oil to a gentle boil and spoon in dough.

To maintain even cooking keep burner on medium.

Fry 3-5 minutes on each side.

Biltong

A delicious stew enhanced with peanut butter.

Makes: 4 servings.

Ingredients:

- 1 tablespoon peanut oil
- 8-10 ounces biltong (or substitute with chicken breast and 2 strips of smoky bacon)
- 1 large onion, diced or julienned
- ½ tbsp garlic
- 1 1/2 teaspoon ginger (freshly grated)
- 1 1/2 tablespoons tomato puree
- 2-3 tablespoons peanut butter
- 2 beefsteak tomatoes, quartered or diced (can substitute with 2 cups diced or crushed canned with no salt, adjust puree ratio accordingly)
- 1 tsp cayenne pepper
- 2/3 cup water

Directions:

To skillet warmed over medium high heat, add onions; garlic; ginger; and sauté 1-2 minutes.

Stir-fry biltong in aromatics 30-40 seconds and then stir in tomato puree and peanut butter. Careful to ensure to biltong gets coated.

For 3-5 minutes stir in quartered or diced tomatoes; stir in cayenne pepper and water.

Cover, reduce heat and simmer 3-5 minutes.

It is assumed the addition of peanut butter is to as a supplement for some of the protein as traditionally biltong is expensive.

West African Inspired Peanut Soup

Usually a scotch bonnet pepper is used and falls in the 80,000-400,00 SHU on the Scoville scale. Substitutes include Thai red chiles and Habanero's.

Makes: 4-6 servings.

Ingredients:

- 1-2 whole onions, peeled
- 2-3 large tomatoes
- 4-6 thighs, legs, and drumsticks
- 7 eggs
- 12-14 okra pods
- 1 pepper
- 1/2-2/3 tbsp ginger, minced or grated
- 2-4 bay leaves
- 5-7 heaping tablespoons natural peanut butter
- 7 ½ -8 cups no salt or low sodium chicken stock

Directions:

In large heavy pot add whole onions, minced ginger, tomatoes.

Sauté 20-30 seconds and add chicken.

If desired, brown it a little before adding in chicken stock then bring to a boil, reduce heat, cover and simmer 20-25 minutes.

Pour into blender and puree (if desired, removed tomato skin with fork)

In a saucepan warmed over medium heat let peanut butter melt.

Add in water ½ tsp at a time until a smooth sauce develops (this process is comparable to the making of a roux).

Once developed add sauce to the pot; peanut oil will separate.

Mix in washed okra and simmer 5-10 minutes.

Kefta Briouat

The famous fried, mildly flavored, pastries of Morocco! Thin dough, warqa, that can be substituted with phyllo dough or spring roll wrappers.

Ingredients:

- 1 lb. ground meat, beef or lamb
- 1 medium onion, diced
- 3/4 teaspoon paprika
- 1 1/4 teaspoon cumin seeds
- 2/3 teaspoon pepper
- 1/2 teaspoons salt
- 1/2 teaspoon cinnamon
- 3 tablespoons butter
- ¼ cup parsley leaves, chopped
- 2 eggs, beaten
- 1 pound or package warqa or thin dough
- 3 tablespoons butter melted
- 2 egg yolk, beaten
- 3 cups vegetable oil

Directions:

In a large skillet warmed over medium high heat, sauté 30 seconds to 1-minute onion, paprika, cumin seeds, pepper, salt, cinnamon and butter.

Add in ground meat, stirring well, and cook till no longer pink.

Add in chopped parsley and eggs. Stirring constantly to incorporate into meat or else will burn.

Remove from heat and set aside or spread out on paper towel lined plate to drain.

Lay out dough, cut into long strips roughly 2 ½ - 3 inches wide.

With pastry brush, brush with melted butter bottom 2/3 of strip and place one spoonful of ground meat in center of dough.

Fold into a triangle shape and fry 2-3 minutes per side or until golden brown.

Make thee ahead! Freeze 2-3 weeks in advance and rehea tin a 350 degree oven 5-10 minutes!

Moroccan Inspired Tagine

Soaking the okra 45 minutes to 1 hr. in water and vinegar helps reduce the 'sliminess' of okra.

Makes: 4-5 servings.

Ingredients:

- 2/3 -1 lb. lamb or beef
- 2/3 -1 lb. okra, trimmed and soaked
- ½ -1 lb. zucchini, chopped
- 4 cups plum tomatoes, quartered
- 1 red onion, diced or julienned
- 1-2 heaping tbsp garlic, minced
- 1 1/2 tablespoons cilantro, chopped or 2-3 tsp toasted coriander seeds
- 1 tablespoons parsley, chopped
- 2/3 tablespoon ginger
- 1/2 teaspoons salt, or to taste
- 2/3 teaspoon pepper
- ¾ teaspoon turmeric
- 1/3 tsp saffron threads
- 3 ½ - 4 cups water

Directions:

In a large pot warmed over medium high heat sauté onions, garlic, cilantro, parsley, ginger, salt, pepper, turmeric, and saffron threads 30-40 seconds.

Add meat and brown.

Stir in water, stirring bring to a boil, reduce heat, cover, and simmer 1 hour and 20 minutes or 80 minutes.

Stir in okra and return to simmer for 8-11 minutes.

Stir in zucchini and simmer 3-4 more minutes.

No Tagine Chicken Tagine

All the Moroccan flavors, plus, a money and space saver!

Makes: 4 servings.

Ingredients:

- 1 tablespoon olive oil
- 4 chicken thighs
- 1 onion, julienned
- 1-2 tsp garlic, minced
- 1 ½ -2 teaspoons ras al hanout, or more to taste.
- 1/2 teaspoon turmeric
- 1/3 teaspoon ground coriander
- Salt and pepper
- 1/2 tablespoon of ginger, minced or grated
- 12-14 dried apricots, halved
- 12 -14 pitted prunes, halved
- 2 cups chicken stock
- parsley for garnish

Directions:

In skillet warmed over medium high heat, brown chicken thighs 5-6 minutes on one side 4-5 minutes on the other.

Transfer to another plate and set aside.

Lower burner to medium and sauté onion, garlic, and ginger.

Stir in ras al hanout, turmeric, coriander, salt and pepper and sauté 30-45 seconds.

Return chicken pieces to pot as well as, apricots, prunes, chicken stock and simmer 35-40 minutes (the longer the better).

This form of tagine is usually served over spicy yellow rice or Sadza.

Okra Pressure Cooker Tagine

Keep the rich depths of African cuisine but in half the time!

Makes: 4 servings.

Ingredients:

- 1/2 -1 lb. lamb or beef
- 1/2 -1 lb. okra, trimmed and soaked
- 2/3 -3/4 lb. zucchini, chopped
- 4 cups plum tomatoes, quartered
- 1 red onion, diced or julienned
- 1-2 heaping tbsp garlic, minced
- 1 1/2 tablespoons cilantro, chopped or 2-3 tsp toasted coriander seeds
- 1 tablespoons parsley, chopped
- 2/3 tablespoon ginger
- 1/2 teaspoons salt, or to taste
- 2/3 teaspoon pepper
- ¾ teaspoon turmeric
- ½ teaspoon red pepper flakes
- 1/3 tsp saffron threads
- 3- 3 ½ cups water

Directions:

Set pressure cooker to sauté and brown meat in onions, garlic, and ginger.

Stir in quartered tomatoes, parsley and cilantro/coriander.

Cover and simmer 5-10 minutes.

Stir in water.

Cover, lock lid, and set to high pressure and cook 20 minutes.

Quick release pressure and set to sauté mode.

Add in okra and simmer 3-4 minutes.

Repeat for zucchini.

Chicken Durban Curry

A fusion of African and Indian!

Makes: 4-6 servings.

Ingredients:

- 1 tablespoon ghee
- 1 tablespoon vegetable oil
- ¾ tablespoon curry powder or garam masala
- 1/2 tablespoon of coriander
- 1 ¼ tablespoon of cumin
- 2/3 teaspoon of cumin seeds
- 2/3 teaspoon of cayenne pepper
- ½ - 1 cinnamon sticks
- 1 onion, chopped
- 1 tbsp ginger, minced
- 2-3 teaspoons garlic, minced
- 4-6 pieces of chicken thighs or legs
- 2-3 plum tomatoes, chopped or quartered
- 1 tablespoon of tomato puree
- 1 1/2 cups potatoes cubes
- ¾ -1 cup of no salt chicken stock

Directions:

In a heavy pot warmed over medium heat melt butter into oil and sauté onions, ginger, garlic 1-2 minutes.

Add curry powder/garam masala, coriander, cumin, cumin seeds, cayenne pepper, cinnamon or stick and sauté 30 seconds to 1 minute.

Increase heat to high and add the chicken, getting as much of the onion-spice mixture on pieces as possible.

Add in potato cubes and stock; bring to a boil, reduce heat and cover, simmer 25-30 minutes.

Sambal (honey glazed Moroccan Carrots)

Serve alone, with a creamy dip, or with feta cheese!

Makes: 2 servings.

Ingredients:

- 1/3 lb. carrots
- ¾ tablespoon olive oil
- ¾ tablespoon honey
- 2/3 teaspoon cumin
- 1/3 teaspoon ginger
- 1/3 teaspoon coriander
- 1/3-1/2 teaspoon cinnamon
- ¼ teaspoon salt
- ¼ teaspoon pepper

Directions:

Preheat oven to 400 and line tray with parchment paper.

In bowl whisk together olive oil, honey, cumin, ginger, coriander, and cinnamon.

Add in carrots and coat well.

Spread out on tray and bake 25-30 minutes.

Lamb Tagine a.k.a Mrouzia Traditional Version

A favorite Moroccan dish!

Makes: 4 servings.

Ingredients:

- 1 lbs. lamb or beef cut into 2 ½ -3 inch chunks
- 1-2 teaspoons Ras El Hanout
- 1 teaspoon ginger, powder
- 1/2 teaspoon salt
- 2/3 teaspoon pepper
- 2/3 teaspoon turmeric
- 1/3 teaspoon saffron threads
- 1 onion minced or grated
- 1-2 teaspoon garlic, minced
- 1 cinnamon stick, halved
- 1 heaping tablespoon butter or ghee
- 2 ½ -3 cups water
- 1 cup dark golden or sultana raisins
- 1/3 cup honey
- ¾ teaspoon cinnamon
- 1/3 – ½ cup almonds

Directions:

In a bowl combine ras el hanout, ginger, salt, pepper, turmeric, with meat chunks and coat well.

In large pot warmed over medium high heat, sauté butter, onions, garlic, cinnamon sticks.

Add meat chunks to pot, reduce heat to medium, cover and cook 8-10 minutes turning once half-way through.

Stir in water and cook 90-120 minutes.

Stir in raisins, honey, and cinnamon. If needed add water 1 tbsp at a time until raisins are just covered.

Cover and simmer 25-30 minutes.

Tagine Cooker Mrouzia

A traditional cooker made of clay!

Makes: 4 servings.

Ingredients:

- 1 lbs. lamb or beef, cut into 3 inch or larger pieces
- 1-2 teaspoons Ras El Hanout
- 1 1/2 teaspoons ginger
- 1/4 teaspoons salt
- 1/2 teaspoon pepper
- 3/4 teaspoon turmeric
- 1/3 teaspoon saffron threads
- 2 medium onions (grated)
- 2 small pieces of cinnamon stick (2 to 3 inches)
- 3 cloves of garlic (pressed or finely chopped)
- 3 cups water
- 1/2 cup unsalted butter
- ¼ -1/2 cup honey
- 1 1/2 cups dark golden or sultana raisins
- 1/3 – 2/3 cup blanched almonds
- 2/3 teaspoon cinnamon

Directions:

In a bowl combine ras el hanout, ginger, salt, pepper, turmeric, saffron threads.

Add in chucks of meat and coat well.

Add to bowl onions, garlic, and cinnamon sticks.

Toss well.

Add butter, meat, and water to tagine then simmer 2 ½ -3 hours on medium-low heat.

Stir in raisins, honey, and cinnamon covering with water if necessary.

Simmer another 20-30 minutes.

Quick Easy Ras El Hanout Spice Mix

This spice mix is so popular it is always on the must-experience lists for Morocco!

Makes: approx. ¼ cup.

Ingredients:

- 1 1/2 teaspoons ground ginger
- 1/2 teaspoon ground cardamom
- 2/3 teaspoons ground mace
- 1/3 teaspoon ground cinnamon
- 1/2 teaspoon ground allspice
- 1/3 teaspoon ground coriander seeds
- 1/3 teaspoon ground nutmeg
- 3/4 teaspoon turmeric
- 1/3 teaspoon ground black pepper
- 1/4 teaspoon ground white pepper
- 1/2 teaspoon ground cayenne pepper
- 1/3 teaspoon ground anise seeds
- 1/4 teaspoon ground cloves

Directions:

In a bowl combine ginger, cardamom, mace, cinnamon, allspice, coriander seeds, nutmeg, turmeric, black pepper, white pepper, cayenne pepper, anise seeds, and cloves.

Whisk together or put lid on bowl and shake repeatedly.

Store in cool, dry place and will keep for several months.

Every version of the Ras El Hanout spice mix varies by a bit, giving each seasoning mix its own unique flavor!

Chickpea Tagine with Carrots

Great vegetarian dish!

Makes: 4 servings.

Ingredients:

- 1 red onion, chopped
- 1 ½ garlic, minced
- 1 tablespoon olive oil
- 1/4 teaspoons salt
- 1 teaspoon ginger, powder
- 3/4 teaspoon turmeric, powder
- 2/3 teaspoon cinnamon
- 1/3 teaspoon black pepper
- 1/3 teaspoon cayenne pepper
- 1/3 teaspoon Ras el hanout (optional)
- 1 -2 tablespoons chopped parsley
- 6 medium sized peeled carrots
- 1 cup no sodium vegetable or chicken broth
- ½-1 tablespoon honey
- 1 can chickpeas, drained
- 1 teaspoon chili pepper, minced
- 1/4 cup golden raisins

Directions:

In bottom of tagine sauté onions and garlic 1-2 minutes.

Over medium-low heat, add in salt, ginger, turmeric, cinnamon, black pepper, cayenne pepper, ras el hanout, parsley, carrots, and water.

Cover and cook until carrots soften and are tender (keep checking and when you can cut them with a fork without much pressure they're done).

Add in honey, raisins, chickpeas, and chili peppers.

Simmer another 5-10 minutes.

Khobz dyal Smida -Moroccan Semolina Bread

Also, used as a basis for making pasta or couscous, semolina or durum flour may be used!

Makes: 2 loaves, 8 servings.

Ingredients:

- 2 cups + 2 tbsp fine semolina grits or durum flour
- 1 1/2cups + 2 tbsp white flour
- 1-2 teaspoons sugar
- 1 1/2 to 2 cups of warm water, approx.
- 1/2 teaspoons salt
- 1 1/4 tablespoon of dry or fresh yeast
- 1 tablespoon vegetable oil
- fine or coarse semolina for dusting the loaves
- additional flour for kneading

Directions:

Prepare 2 baking trays with baking non-stick spray and preheat oven to 435.

In a bowl combine semolina, flour, salt, sugar.

With finger make a small well in the center and add yeast.

Add oil and water to the well and stir yeast until dissolved. Slowly extending outward to include flour.

On a floured surface knead dough up to 10 minutes adding water ½ tsp at a time if needed.

Divide and flatten each portion into a disc shape then place on baking trays and let sit 10 minutes.

Dough will rise slightly, press back down and re-form into round, disc shape; cover with towel and let sit 1 hr. in a cool, dry place.

Using large fork poke some vent holes into dough and bake 20 minutes.

Unfortunately, this bread only keeps for 1 day. For leftovers, freeze immediately after eating! Thaw the leftovers to room temp and oven re-heat!

Khobz- Moroccan White Bread

A.k.a. by its French name, force.

Makes: 2 loaves- 8 servings.

Ingredients:

- 4 cups flour high-gluten or bread flour
- 1 teaspoons salt
- 1-2 teaspoons sugar
- ¾ tablespoon + 4 teaspoons active dry yeast
- 1 1/2 tablespoons vegetable oil
- 1 1/3 cups warm water

Directions:

Preheat oven to 435 and prepare 2 baking sheets.

In a bowl mix together flour, salt, sugar.

Using fingers make a well in center of dough, fill with oil and water.

Still with fingers mix water and yeast together until yeast dissolves.

Slowly extend mixing out to include flour.

Place dough on floured surface, knead up to 10 minutes. If needed, add water 1/2 tsp at a time.

Divide dough equally, place in bowls, cover, and set in cool, dry place for 12-15 minutes.

Form dough into then disc, return to bowls and let rise 60-80 minutes.

Using fork, puncture dough to allow steam to escape, and bake 20 minutes.

Easy Vegetable Ragu Over Couscous

Many like this dish topped with tfaya, a delicious onion raisin mix!

Makes: 4 servings.

Ingredients:

- 1/4 tsp salt
- 1 tbsp butter
- 1 cabbage, cut into 6 chunks
- 2-3 turnips, peeled and sliced
- 6-8 carrots, peeled and sliced
- 1 large tomato, peeled and quartered
- 1 onion, halved
- 2/3 can fava beans
- 1/2 -1 tbsp jalapeño or chili peppers
- 2 cups cubes acorn squash – or cubes of butternut squash
- 3-4 zucchini, halved and sliced
- 1 -2 cups sweet potatoes mash
- 2-3 cups of beef or vegetable stock

Directions:

In large pot over medium heat, add salt, butter and onion and swirl around area to season it.

If you are cooking meat now is the time. When finished transfer to plate to drain but leave some grease in pot.

Add in cabbage, turnips, and carrots. Sauté 1-2 minutes.

Add in quartered tomatoes and sauté 30 seconds.

Add in squash cubes, sweet potato mash, stock, jalapeno's, fava beans. If adding meat put it now.

Bring to boil, reduce heat, cover, let simmer 40-60 minutes.

Meanwhile cook couscous as directed and serve chicken over it.

Tfaya

Great over everything from meats to roasted veggies!

Makes: 2 servings.

Ingredients:

- ¾ cup raisins
- 2 1/2 cup onions, julienned
- 2-3 tablespoons butter
- 3-4 tablespoons honey
- 2/3 teaspoon pepper
- 1/2 teaspoon cinnamon
- 3/4 teaspoon ginger
- 1/3 teaspoon turmeric
- 1/3 teaspoon saffron threads (crumbled)
- Pinch of salt
- 1/3 -1/2 cup water
- 1 – 1 1/2 tablespoons orange flower water or rose water

Directions:

In bowl, soak raisins in water 20-30 minutes.

In skillet warmed over medium high heat melt butter and sauté onions 2-3 minutes.

Drain raisins.

To pot add drained raisins, butter, honey, pepper, cinnamon, ginger, turmeric, saffron, salt, and water.

Bring mixture to a boil, reduce heat, cover, and simmer 25-30 minutes.

Stir in flower water and let thicken to desired consistency.

Onion Mezgueldi

Ingredients:

- 2 lbs. onions, sliced
- 1/3 cup vegetable oil
- 1 tablespoon sugar
- 1 teaspoons cinnamon
- 2/3 teaspoon ginger
- 1/3 – 2/3 teaspoon turmeric
- Pinch of salt
- ½ to 1 tsp coarse black pepper
- ¼ tsp saffron threads

Directions:

In bowl combine sugar, cinnamon, ginger, turmeric, salt, pepper, saffron threads.

Gently mix onions into spice mix. Taking care to keep as much of the ring in tacked as possible.

Transfer onions to skillet or tagine warmed over medium high heat, cover, and cook 60-90 minutes.

You can also bake these onions! Bake at 375 60-90 minutes.

Mezgueldi M'chermel

Another delicious topping mixture for proteins, veggies, couscous, etc.!

Makes: 2 servings.

Ingredients:

- 3-4 cups onion slices
- 1-2 tbsp oil
- 1-2 teaspoons ginger
- 2/3 teaspoon sweet paprika
- 1/2 teaspoon cumin
- 1/3 teaspoon turmeric
- 1/3 teaspoon salt
- 1/3 teaspoon cayenne pepper (or black pepper)
- 1/3 saffron threads
- 1/3-inch-piece of cinnamon stick

Directions:

In bowl combine ginger, sweet paprika, cumin, turmeric, salt, cayenne pepper, saffron threads.

Gently mix onions into spice mix. Taking care to keep as much of the ring in tacked as possible.

Transfer onions to skillet or tagine warmed over medium high heat, cover, and cook 60-90 minutes.

Pressure Cooker Stewed Lentils

This dish can turn anyone into a lentil lover. Lamb, ground beef or bacon are just a few great additions!

Makes: 4-5 servings.

Ingredients:

- 2 1/2cups brown or green lentils
- 1 10 oz. can stew tomatoes
- 1 tsp turmeric, minced (optional)
- 1 red onion, grated or julienned
- ½ tablespoon turmeric, minced or grated
- 2 tsp garlic, minced
- 4 tablespoons parsley, diced
- 1 bay leaf, crushed
- 1 teaspoon toasted cumin seeds
- 2 teaspoons smoked paprika
- 2/3 teaspoon sweet ginger
- ¼ teaspoon ginger
- 1/2 teaspoon coarse black pepper
- ½ tsp cayenne pepper
- 1/3 tablespoon clove
- 8 cups water

Directions:

In a pressure cooker combine lentils, tomatoes, onion, turmeric, garlic, parsley, crushed bay leaf, toasted cumin seeds, smoked paprika, sweet ginger, ginger, pepper, cayenne pepper, clove.

Set cooker to sauté and toast spices 30 seconds or until fragrant.

Add in lentils water, close lid, lock, set to high pressure and cook 30 minutes.

Easy African Stove Top Lentils and Okra

Another great savory hearty dish that's good as the main entree or to enhance a main dish!

Makes: approx. 4 cups.

Ingredients:

- 4-4 1/2 cups brown or green lentils
- 3-5 pieces of okra, sliced -soaked in water and vinegar to reduce sliminess
- 2 10 oz. cans stewed tomatoes
- 1 tablespoon butter or ghee
- 1 ½ tsp turmeric, minced (optional)
- 1 red onion, grated or julienned
- 2 tsp garlic, minced
- 4 tablespoons parsley, diced
- 1 bay leaf, crushed
- 1 teaspoon toasted cumin seeds
- 2/3 teaspoons sweet paprika
- 3/4 teaspoon smoked paprika
- 1/3 teaspoon ginger
- 1/3 teaspoon coarse black pepper
- 1/3 tsp chili pepper or cayenne pepper
- 1/4 tablespoon cinnamon
- 8 cups water, beef, or vegetable stock

Directions:

In pot warmed over high heat, melt butter and sauté turmeric, onion, and garlic 1-2 minutes.

Stir in parsley, crushed bay leaf, toasted cumin seeds, sweet paprika, smoked paprika, pepper,

Chili pepper/cayenne pepper, cinnamon and stir fry 30-40 seconds or until room is fragrant and bottom of pot is seasoned.

Pour in water or stock, bring to a boil, reduce heat, cover, let simmer 35-45 minutes.

Easy Ground Beef Lentil Veggie Stew

Served over spicy yellow couscous or creamy mashed potatoes!

Makes: 4 servings.

Ingredients:

- ½ -1 lbs., ground beef
- 1 package or 4 cups dried brown or green lentils
- 1 24 oz. can crushed or stewed tomatoes
- 2 cups carrots, sliced (can substitute with sweet potatoes, any root vegetable or hearty squash)
- 1 tablespoon turmeric, minced
- ½ onion, chopped, grated or julienned
- 1 ½ tsp garlic, minced
- 2 bay leaves
- ¾ teaspoon cumin
- 1/2 teaspoon smoked paprika
- 2/3 teaspoon sweet paprika
- ¼ teaspoon sweet ginger
- 1/2 teaspoon cinnamon
- ¼ tsp cayenne pepper
- 1/4 tablespoon clove
- 8 cups water

Directions:

In large pot brown ground beef, transfer to paper towel lined plated to drain.

Keep some hamburger grease in bottom of pot. (Some prefer stew with all of the grease in the stew, if you do too skip this step)

In grease melt butter and sauté onions, turmeric, and garlic.

Add in bay leaves, cumin, smoked paprika, sweet paprika, sweet ginger, cinnamon, cayenne pepper, clove.

Stir in liquid.

Bring to a boil, reduce heat, cover, simmer 30-50 minutes.

Harira

A traditional stew that's handed down through the generations!

Makes: 4-6 servings.

Ingredients:

- 2/3-pound lamb or beef
- 1 tablespoons butter or ghee
- 3 cups water
- 1/3 cup dried lentils
- 1 cup tomato sauce
- 2/3 tablespoon tomato paste
- 2 ½ -3 tablespoons water
- 1/3 tablespoon cinnamon
- 1 teaspoon ginger
- 2/3 teaspoon turmeric
- 1/3 cup cilantro, chopped
- ¾ cup parsley, chopped
- 1 large onion (grated)
- ½ cup celery, diced
- 2 cups chickpeas-soaked in water 45-60 minutes
- 5-6 large tomatoes
- 1 ½ cup water or no sodium chicken stock

Directions:

Preheat oven to 300 and prepare 9x9 pan.

Chop tomatoes in half, wrap in aluminum foil, drizzle with olive oil, close but leave room for hot air to escape, put in dish and cook 15-20 minutes or until soft.

Slip skin off with fork and transfer tomatoes to processor and puree. Set aside.

Warm pot over medium high heat add oil and butter/ghee then sauté tomato paste, cinnamon, ginger, turmeric, cilantro, parsley, celery, onions, and stir-fry 2-3 minutes.

In large pot over medium high heat add oil and brown meat.

Stir in water, lentils, chickpeas, water or stock.

Bring to a boil, reduce heat, cover, simmer 45-55 minutes.

20 Minute Pressure Cooker Harira

Add in seasonal root vegetables!

Makes: 4-6 servings.

Ingredients:

- 3-4 cups shredded chicken
- 1 1/2 tablespoons vegetable oil
- 1 tablespoon butter or ghee
- 3 /2 - 4 cups water
- 2/3 cup tomato sauce
- 3/4 tablespoon tomato paste
- 1/2 tablespoon cinnamon
- 1/3 teaspoon ginger
- 1/3 teaspoon turmeric
- 1/3 cup coriander seeds
- ¾ cup parsley, chopped
- ½ cup mire poix
- ½ cup lentils, green or brown
- 2 cups chickpeas-soaked in water 45-60 minutes
- 5-6 large tomatoes
- 4-6 tablespoons water (depends on how thick you like your gravy)
- 2 cups no sodium chicken stock

Directions:

Set pressure cooker to sauté and melt butter into oil and sauté mire poix, parsley, coriander seeds, turmeric, ginger, cinnamon, tomato paste, tomato sauce, lentils, chickpeas, water, broth 1 minute.

Close, lock lid, set to high, and cook 20 minutes.

Lamb Harira Over Yellow Couscous

Great for casual occasions!

Makes: 4 servings.

Ingredients:

- ½ lbs. lamb
- 1 cup washed and drained peas and carrots
- 2/3 tablespoons vegetable oil
- ½ heaping tablespoon butter or ghee
- 3 cups water
- 1/3 cup tomato sauce
- ¼ tablespoon tomato paste
- 2/3 tablespoon cinnamon
- 1/4 teaspoon ginger
- 1/4 teaspoon sweet paprika
- ¼ teaspoon chili pepper
- ¼ teaspoon cumin seeds
- 2/3 teaspoon cloves
- ½ teaspoon fennel seeds
- ¾ cup cilantro
- ½ cup mire poix
- ½ cup lentils, green or brown
- 2 cups chickpeas-soaked in water 45-60 minutes
- 5-6 large tomatoes
- 4-6 tablespoons water (depends on how thick you like your gravy)
- 2 cups no sodium chicken stock

Directions:

Set pressure cooker to sauté and melt butter into oil and sauté mire poix, cilantro, fennel seeds, cloves, cumin seeds, chili pepper, ginger, cinnamon, tomato paste, tomato sauce, lentils, chickpeas, water, broth 1 minute.

Add in lamb meat, carrots, and peas.

Close, lock lid, set to high, and cook 20 minutes.

Make yellow couscous as package directs.

Serve Harira over couscous with hot garlic naan bread!

Kalinti

A popular quiche like dish made of chickpea flour.

Makes: 4 servings.

Ingredients:

- 1 3/4 cups chickpea flour
- 1 2/3 teaspoons baking powder
- Pinch of salt (optional)
- 1/4 teaspoon pepper
- 1/3 teaspoon cumin
- ¼ teaspoon cayenne pepper (if using reduce black pepper to ¼ teaspoon.)
- 1/3 teaspoon cloves or cinnamon
- 1/3- 2/3 cup milk (or 2 cups water)
- 2 egg whites
- 1 egg yolk
- 1/2 cup vegetable oil

Directions:

Preheat oven to 375-400 and prepare casserole dish.

In large bowl combine flour, baking powder, pinch of salt, pepper, cumin, cayenne pepper, cloves.

Whisk in milk or water, egg whites, yolk, oil.

Beat well and pour into dish.

Bake 40-50 minutes.

Easy Harissa Spice Mix

Although dried red chili peppers are the standard, any heat level will work.

Makes: approx. 1 cup.

Ingredients:

- 5 cups water
- 4 peppers, chopped
- 2/3 tablespoon butter
- 5 cloves roasted garlic or 2 tbsp minced garlic
- 1 teaspoon turmeric, minced (optional)
- 1 teaspoon ginger, minced (optional)
- 1/3 teaspoon black pepper
- 1/3 teaspoon cumin
- 2/3 tablespoon lemon juice

Directions:

Boil peppers in water until soft.

Chop.

In medium sized pot melt butter and sauté garlic, turmeric, and ginger.

Stir in softened chopped chili peppers. Stir well.

Stir in black pepper, cumin, and lemon juice.

Simmer 5-10 minutes and remove from heat.

Let cool and transfer to metal or glass bowl then store in refrigerator

With time the flavors will meld and get hotter.

When serving time, reheat over medium heat.

Spoon into or beside all sorts of dishes for and extra dollop of wow!

Stew Beef Merguez

Traditionally served with sausage!

Makes: 4 servings.

Ingredients:

- ½ -1 lbs. stew beef
- ½ tablespoon butter or ghee
- 1 tablespoon vegetable oil
- 2/3 tablespoon garlic, minced or grated
- 1 teaspoon harissa
- 1/3 – 2/3 tablespoon merguez spice mix
- 1-2 tablespoons diced cilantro (optional)

Directions:

In a large bowl mix together harissa, merguez spice mix, and cilantro.

Toss in stew meat, coating pieces well.

Warm pot over medium high heat and melt butter/ghee into oil.

Sauté garlic 30 seconds to 1 minute.

Add in coated meat pieces and cook 2-3 minutes per side or until browned.

Ground Beef Merguez Stew

Ingredients:

- ½ -3/4 lbs. ground beef or lamb
- ½ tablespoon butter or ghee
- 2/3 cup mire poix
- 3/4 tablespoon garlic, roasted minced
- 1 teaspoon harissa
- ½ tablespoon merguez spice mix
- 1/3 cup no salt added beef broth or water
- 1-2 tablespoons diced parsley

Directions:

In large pot warmed over medium high heat, brown ground beef or lamb.

Remove from pot to a paper towel lined plate to drain.

Leave a little protein grease in the pot. For added flavoring try adding in bacon grease or 1 piece of fatback.

Add butter or ghee to pot and let melt in grease, sautéing around pot to season.

Sauté garlic, mire poix, merguez spice mix and harissa.

Stir in browned and drained protein.

Bring to a boil, reduce heat, cover, simmer 15-20 minutes.

Top with parsley before serving.

Easy Homemade Merguez Spice Mixture

For extra sweetness add in some glucose powder.

Makes: approx. ½-2/3 cup.

Ingredients:

- 1 tablespoon cumin seeds
- 3/4 tablespoon fennel seeds
- 1 tablespoon coriander seeds
- 2 tablespoons paprika
- 2 tablespoons salt
- 2/3 teaspoon pepper
- 1 teaspoon cinnamon
- 1 teaspoon chili powder or cayenne pepper

Directions:

Combine sweet paprika, fennel seeds, cumin seeds, coriander seeds, salt, pepper, cinnamon, chili pepper or cayenne pepper.

Store in airtight container in cool, dry place.

Zesty Chicken with Fried Almonds

Sometimes chicken cubes are served over couscous, lentils, or collard green/spinach sadza!

Makes: 4 servings.

Ingredients:

- 1 whole chicken cut into pieces or 4 boneless, skinless chicken breasts
- 2/3 -1 cup almonds, sliced or crushed
- ¾ tablespoon butter or ghee
- 1 tablespoon vegetable oil
- 1 onion, diced or julienned
- 1/2 teaspoon fennel seeds
- 2/3 teaspoon cumin (powder)
- ¼ teaspoon turmeric (powder)
- ½ teaspoon sweet paprika
- 1/3 teaspoon sweet ginger
- 2 bay leaves
- ½ tablespoon butter
- 1 -1 ½ cup chicken stock
- Any vegetables such as carrots, okra, etc. (optional)
- ¾ - 1 cup rice

Directions:

In large pot over medium high heat, melt butter into oil then add diced or julienned onions, fennel seeds, cumin, turmeric, sweet paprika, and stir-fry 1 minute or until really fragrant.

Add in almonds and sauté 1 minute then set aside, let drain and cool.

Add in ghee, chicken pieces or breasts.

Brown 1-2 minutes pour in stock, vegetables, and rice kernels.

Moroccan Inspired Vegetable Soup

A savory, hearty comfort food for fall days!

Makes: 4 servings.

Ingredients:

- 8-10 carrots- washed, peeled, and cut in half
- 3-4 cups cubed zucchini
- 3-4 cubes cubed sweet potatoes
- 3-4 sliced and soaked okra (soak for 1 hr. in a 50-50 blend of water and vinegar to remove sliminess)
- 3-4 green chilies or jalapenos (optional)- if too hot try green bell pepper
- 2 tablespoons butter or ghee
- ½ tablespoon vegetable oil
- 1 piece of ginger- thinly sliced
- 1 piece of turmeric, thinly sliced
- 2 chopped onions
- ½ teaspoon black cumin seeds
- ½ teaspoon fennel seeds
- 1/3 teaspoon cloves
- 2/3 teaspoon chili or cayenne powder
- ½ teaspoon cinnamon
- 4 cups no alt beef broth or stock
- Salt and pepper to taste
- Parsley, chopped for garnish

Directions:

In a large pot over medium high heat melt butter or ghee into oil then sauté ginger, turmeric, and onion for 1 minute.

Add in black cumin seeds, fennel seeds, cloves, chili pepper or cayenne pepper, cinnamon and sauté 30-40 seconds.

Add in prepared vegetables. Brown if desired.

Stir in broth, adding salt and pepper as needed.

Top with parsley before serving.

Store leftovers in airtight container in refrigerator and will keep 3-4 days.

Freeze soup up to 1 month.

African Inspired Sweet Potato Chicken Soup

You'll love this thick and hearty stew!

Makes: 4 servings.

Ingredients:

- 3-4 cups shredded chicken or ground beef
- 3-4 large sweet potatoes- washed, peeled, and cubed (sweet potato spirals work too)
- 1 tablespoon butter or ghee
- 2 large sweet white onions (chopped)
- 1-piece ginger, minced or grated
- 1-piece turmeric, minced or grated
- 1/2 teaspoons salt
- ½ teaspoons white pepper
- 1/3 teaspoon black pepper
- 1/4 teaspoon cloves
- 1/2 teaspoon saffron threads
- 1/4 tablespoon cinnamon
- 1/3 tablespoon smoked paprika
- ¾ cup no sodium chicken stock or beef stock

Directions:

In large pot warmed over medium high heat melt butter then sauté ginger, turmeric, and onion 2-4 minutes. (another option is to let them sweat 20 minutes over low heat)

Add in salt, both peppers, cloves, saffron threads, cinnamon, smoked paprika and stir-fry 30-40 seconds.

Stir in chicken and sweet potatoes; coating both in spices.

Letting sweet potatoes brown on the edges.

Stir in broth, bring to boil, reduce heat, cover, let simmer 20-25 minutes.

Moroccan Beef Stew

Great leftover meat for tacos!

Makes: 4-6 servings.

Ingredients:

- 1 3-5 lbs. beef roast
- 1 tablespoon butter or ghee
- 1 tablespoon olive oil
- 2 large sweet white onions (chopped)
- 1 teaspoon minced garlic
- 1/3 tablespoon ginger
- ½ teaspoon turmeric
- 1/3 teaspoon salt
- 1/3 tablespoon cumin seeds
- 2/3easpoon chili or cayenne pepper
- 1 teaspoon black pepper
- 1 teaspoon cloves
- 1 teaspoon saffron threads
- 2/3 teaspoon cinnamon
- 1-2 cups beef stock
- 1 bunch parsley for garnish

Directions:

In a big pot over the medium high heat, melt butter into olive oil and sauté garlic and onions for 30-50 seconds.

Add in ginger, turmeric, salt, cumin seeds, chili or cayenne pepper, black pepper, cloves, saffron threads, cinnamon and sauté another 30-40 seconds or until fragrant.

Add in beef and brown 3-5 minutes.

Pour in stock; bring to a boil, reduce heat, cover, simmer 20-30 minutes.

Moroccan Inspired Beef Stew for the Crock Pot

Serve over mashed potatoes or rice!

Makes: 4-6 servings.

Ingredients:

- 1 3-5 lbs. beef roast
- 1 tablespoon butter or ghee
- 1 tablespoon olive oil
- 10-20 pearl onions
- 2/3 teaspoon garlic, minced or grated
- 1/2 tablespoon ginger, minced or gated
- 2/3 teaspoon turmeric, minced or grated
- Salt and pepper to taste
- 1/4 tablespoon cumin
- 1/4 teaspoon chili pepper
- 1/3 teaspoon smoked paprika
- ¼ teaspoon cloves
- 1/2 teaspoon saffron threads
- 1/2 teaspoon cinnamon
- 1 cup sliced carrots
- 1 cup sliced okra
- 1 cup chunked sweet potato
- 4-6 cups beef stock

Directions:

In bottom of crockpot turned onto low melt butter into oil and swirl around applying thin layer to bowl.

Add in onions, garlic, ginger, and turmeric pushing back and forth and around 30 sec. – 1 minute seasoning the bowl.

Sprinkle over them salt and pepper, cumin, chili pepper, smoked paprika, cloves, saffron threads, cinnamon and sauté until very fragrant (approx. 30-45 seconds).

Add vegetables and brown 45 seconds to 1 minute, coating well in seasoning.

Add in beef and brown 3-5 minutes.

Pour in stock and cook on high 6-7 hours.

African Inspired Pork Carnita Meat

Great with naan bread!

Makes: 6-10 servings.

Ingredients:

- 1 3-5 lbs. pork butt roast
- 1 tablespoon butter or ghee
- 1/2 tablespoon olive oil
- 2/3 cup onions, diced
- 1 /2 teaspoon minced garlic
- 1 tablespoon ginger, minced
- ½ teaspoon turmeric, minced
- 1 teaspoon jalapeno, minced
- 1/2 tablespoon cumin seeds
- 1/2 teaspoon chili pepper
- 1/2 teaspoon cayenne pepper
- 1/3 teaspoon cloves
- 1/2 teaspoon saffron threads
- 1/3 teaspoon cinnamon
- 1/3 teaspoon chicken bouillon
- 4-5 cups chicken stock
- 1 cup finely diced parsley
- Salt pepper to taste

Directions:

In pot warmed over medium heat, sauté onions, garlic, ginger, turmeric, jalapeno 1-2 minutes.

Add in cumin seeds, chilli pepper, cayenne pepper, cloves, saffron threads, cinnamon, and chicken bouillon. And sauté 40-45 seconds.

Add in stock and bring to boil.

Reduce heat, cover, simmer 20-25 minutes then shred.

Simmer another 7-10 minutes.

It's done when meat is no longer pink or running unclear juices. EATING UNDERCOOKED PORK IS HAZARDOUS FOR YOUR HEALTH.

Crockpot Tandoori Pork Carnita Meat

Feast like never before!

Makes: 1 3-5 lbs. pork butt or shoulder.

Ingredients:

- 1 3-5 lbs. pork butt or shoulder
- 2 tbsp salt
- 4-5 cups water
- 2-3 cups ice cubes
- 1 tablespoon butter or ghee
- 1 1/2-inch piece of ginger, minced or grated
- ½ teaspoon black cumin seeds
- 1-2-star anise
- 2 whole cloves
- ½ teaspoon cinnamon
- ¼ teaspoon turmeric or sweet paprika
- 1/3 teaspoon chicken bouillon
- ½ teaspoon garlic powder with diced parsley
- 1/3 teaspoon jalapeno powder
- 1 can diced tomatoes and green chilies
- 5 cups chicken stock

Directions:

Trim pork of unwanted fat and skin.

Wash and pat dry pork.

Place pork in a large bowl with salt, ice, and water.

Cover and refrigerate 2-4 hours then discard water and pat dry pork.

Sitting out, bring to room temperature.

In crockpot over low heat, melt butter/ghee.

Add in and sauté 1-2 minutes black cumin seeds, star anise, turmeric or sweet paprika, chicken bouillon, garlic powder with parsley, jalapeno powder.

Brown pork in spices.

Press cloves into meat.

Add in tomatoes and chilies and chicken stock.

Cook on high 5-6 hours.

Checking frequently for adequate liquid levels.

Savory Spicy Beef

Easy crockpot meal for serving over rice or mashed potatoes!

Makes: 1 3-5 roast

Ingredients:

- 1 3-5 lbs. beef roast
- 1 can diced tomatoes and green chilies
- 1 tablespoon butter or ghee
- 1 piece of ginger, minced or grated
- ½ teaspoon cumin seeds
- ½ teaspoon fennel seeds
- ¼ tablespoon cinnamon
- ½ teaspoon chili powder
- ¼ teaspoon paprika
- ¼ tablespoon chicken bouillon
- 1/3 teaspoon garlic powder with diced parsley
- ¼ teaspoon jalapeno powder (optional)
- 4-6 cups vegetable or chicken stock

Directions:

In crockpot over low heat melt butter or ghee and sauté ginger 30 seconds to 1 minute.

Mix in cumin seeds, fennel seeds, cinnamon, chili powder, paprika, chicken bouillon, jalapeno powder.

Add in beef and brown 3-4 minutes.

Pour in broth and cook on high 5-6 hours.

Crockpot Taquitos

Recycle your leftovers!

Makes: 8 taquitos.

Ingredients:

- 1 3-5 lbs. beef roast
- 8 8-inch corn or flour tortillas
- 1 tablespoon butter or ghee
- 1 piece of ginger, minced or grated
- ¾ piece turmeric, minced or grated
- ½ teaspoon cumin seeds
- 1/3 teaspoon fennel seeds
- ¼ tablespoon cinnamon
- 1/3 teaspoon chili powder
- 1/3 teaspoon paprika
- ¼ teaspoon chicken bouillon
- 1/4 tablespoon garlic powder with diced parsley
- ¼ tablespoon jalapeno powder
- 4-6 cups vegetable or chicken stock
- 2 eggs
- 1 ½ cup water
- Vegetable oil for frying

Directions:

In crockpot over low heat melt butter or ghee and sauté ginger 30 seconds to 1 minute.

Mix in cumin seeds, fennel seeds, cinnamon, chili powder, paprika, chicken bouillon, jalapeno powder.

Add in beef and brown 3-4 minutes.

Pour in broth and cook on high 5-6 hours then shred.

On a dry surface layout out tortillas.

Mix eggs and water together.

Near edge make a line of shredded beef going down tortilla, roll.

Brush entire taquito with eggwash paying close attention to seal. Always lay taquitos seal side down when not in use.

Bring pot or deep skillet with 2-3 inches of oil to gentle boil.

Slip in 2-4 at a time without crowding, moving every few seconds to ensure even frying.

2-3 minutes or until golden brown.

Moroccan Crockpot Burritos

Excellent way to recycle leftover beef!

Makes: 4 servings.

Ingredients:

- ½ lbs. ground beef
- 4 8-10-inch corn or flour tortillas
- ½ piece garlic, minced or grated
- ½ piece turmeric, minced or grated
- ¼ tablespoon cinnamon
- 1/2 teaspoon smoked paprika
- 1/3 teaspoon harissa
- 1/3 teaspoon cloves
- ½ cup water
- Crumbled and feta cheese
- Chopped parsley
- Olive oil non-stick cooking spray

Directions:

In pot add in ground beef, garlic, and turmeric.

Mix in cinnamon, smoked paprika, harissa, cloves.

Drain hamburger on paper towel lined plate 3-5 minutes.

On a dry surface layout out tortillas, line spoonful of drained burger down tortilla just left of center, fold over and tuck in ends.

Seal edge with water.

Spray crockpot.

Line up burritos, seal side down.

Cook on high 30 minutes.

Transfer to plates, top with cheese and parsley.

Moroccan Chicken Pizza

Great for the younger crowd! Perfect for tailoring to diets while retaining that savory kick!

Makes: 8-10 slices.

Ingredients:

- 1 pizza shell 8-10 inch
- 2 cups thin slices of chicken
- 1 tablespoon butter or ghee
- 2/3 tablespoon olive oil
- 1 sweet onion, julienned
- ½ tablespoon garlic, minced or grated
- 1-2 green chilies, thinly sliced, minced, or grated (chipotle peppers work good too in a pinch!)
- ½-inch piece ginger paste
- 1-inch piece tomato paste
- 1/3 teaspoon turmeric
- ½ teaspoon cumin
- 2/3 teaspoon paprika
- 1/3 teaspoon black pepper
- 1 can crushed or stewed tomatoes
- 1 tub crumbled feta cheese or white cheddar cheese
- 1 bunch parsley, chopped

Directions:

Preheat oven to 400.

In skillet melt butter/ghee into oil.

Sauté onion, garlic, and chilies 1 minute.

Add in ginger paste, turmeric paste, turmeric, cumin, paprika, black pepper and sauté 1 minute.

Pour in tomatoes and stir well.

Bring to a boil, reduce heat, cover and simmer 5-10 minutes.

Remove from heat and let cool.

With shell on pizza round, start topping it by spooning cooled chicken tomato sauce.

After spreading sauce around the shell, top with cheese and parsley.

Cook 8-11 minutes.

46 One Pot Chicken Harissa

Great for a busy, or tired, night!

Makes: 4 servings

Ingredients:

- 4 boneless, skinless chicken breasts or wing and thighs
- 2/3 tablespoon oil or non0stick olive oil spray
- 1 sweet onion, julienned
- 2/3 teaspoon cumin
- ½ teaspoon garlic powder
- ¼ cup mild Moroccan red pepper sauce (in lieu of sauce add ¼ cup red peppers, 1/3 teaspoon coriander, ½ teaspoon paprika, ½ teaspoon lemon juice)
- 1 can diced tomatoes and green chilies

Directions:

In large skillet warmed over medium high, spray then add onion and let cook 5 minutes.

Stir in cumin, garlic powder, and red pepper sauce or ingredients for harissa, and sauté 1 minute.

Add in chicken breast, cooking 4-5 minutes per side.

Add in tomatoes.

Bring to a boil, reduce heat, cover, and simmer 25-30 minutes.

If desired top with crumbled feta!

Harissa Inspired Chicken Lettuce Wraps

A great way to turn leftovers into a light lunch!

Makes: 2 servings.

Ingredients:

- 1 cup shredded harissa meat (see recipe)
- 2 large lettuce leaves
- 1/3 -1/2 cup mayonnaise
- ½ -1 tablespoon ginger, minced
- ½ -1 tablespoon turmeric minced or grated
- ½ -1 tablespoon ginger, minced or grated
- 1-2 tablespoon slivered almonds
- ¼ cup parsley, finely diced

Directions:

In a bowl mix together harissa meat, mayonnaise, ginger, turmeric, ginger, almonds, and parsley.

Spoon into lettuce leaf and roll.

Crockpot Shredded Harissa Meat

Makes great BBQ sandwiches!

Makes: 4-7 servings.

Ingredients:

- 1 whole chicken
- 1/2 tablespoon oil or non-stick olive oil spray
- 1-piece ginger, minced or grated
- 1-piece turmeric, minced or grated
- 2/3 teaspoon cumin
- ½ teaspoon cloves or cinnamon
- ½ teaspoon garlic powder
- 3-4 tablespoons Moroccan red pepper sauce (in lieu of sauce add ¼ cup red peppers, 1/3 teaspoon coriander, ½ teaspoon paprika, ½ teaspoon lemon juice)
- 3-4 cups chicken

Directions:

In bottom of crockpot on low melt butter/ghee then and ginger, turmeric, cumin, cloves or cinnamon, garlic powder, red pepper sauce or ingredients.

Add in chicken and brown and coat with seasoning.

Pour stock down the side of crockpot so not to disturb seasoning on chicken and cook on high 1-2 hours and shred.

Chicken should not be pink or running any unclear juices, eating undercooked chicken is hazardous to your health.

Harissa Fried Shrimp

Also, great recipe for fresh cod!

Makes: 12 shrimp.

Ingredients:

- 12 large shrimp, cleaned
- 3 eggs, beaten
- 1 cup flour
- 2-3 cups panko
- ½ tablespoon onion powder
- 2/3 teaspoon cumin
- ½ teaspoon garlic powder
- 1/3 tablespoon red peppers flakes
- 1/2 teaspoon coriander
- 1/3 teaspoon sweet paprika
- ½ teaspoon lemon peel
- 2/3 teaspoon black pepper
- Vegetable oil

Directions:

Prepare area with three bowls.

In the 1st bowl put flour, in the 2nd bowl place beaten eggs, in the 3rd place the panko.

Whisk into the flour onion powder, garlic powder, cumin, red pepper flakes, coriander, sweet paprika, lemon peel, black pepper.

Bring 2-3 inches of oil to a gentle bowl.

Dip shrimp into bowl 1 then 2 then three.

Let fry 3-5 minutes or until golden brown.

Drain on paper towel lined plate 1-2 minutes before serving.

Harissa Inspired Beef Ribs

Equally good on pork ribs!

Makes: 1 slab beef ribs.

Ingredients:

- 1 slab ribs
- Olive oil for drizzling
- 2/3 tablespoon cumin
- ½ tablespoon sweet paprika
- 1/3 tablespoon garlic powder
- ½ teaspoon turmeric
- 1 teaspoon fennel seeds
- ¼ tablespoon cloves

Directions:

Preheat oven to 400.

Layout ribs.

Drizzle with olive oil and spread on both sides.

In a bowl mix together cumin, sweet paprika, garlic powder, turmeric, fennel seeds, cloves.

Rub spice mix into meat then cover with tin foil.

Cook 30-45 minutes.

Author's Afterthoughts

Thanks ever so much to each of my cherished readers for investing the time to read this book!

I know you could have picked from many other books, but you chose this one. So, a big thanks for reading all the way to the end. If you enjoyed this book or received value from it, I'd like to ask you for a favor. Please take a few minutes to **post an honest and heartfelt review on** *Amazon.com*. Your support does make a difference and helps to benefit other people.

Thanks!

Julia Chiles

About the Author

Julia Chiles

(1951-present)

Julia received her culinary degree from Le Counte' School of Culinary Delights in Paris, France. She enjoyed cooking more than any of her former positions. She lived in Montgomery, Alabama most of her life. She married Roger

Chiles and moved with him to Paris as he pursued his career in journalism. During the time she was there, she joined several cooking groups to learn the French cuisine, which inspired her to attend school and become a great chef.

Julia has achieved many awards in the field of food preparation. She has taught at several different culinary schools. She is in high demand on the talk show circulation, sharing her knowledge and recipes. Julia's favorite pastime is learning new ways to cook old dishes.

Julia is now writing cookbooks to add to her long list of achievements. The present one consists of favorite recipes as well as a few culinary delights from other cultures. She expands everyone's expectations on how to achieve wonderful dishes and not spend a lot of money. Julia firmly believes a wonderful dish can be prepare out of common household staples.

If anyone is interested in collecting Julia's cookbooks, check out your local bookstores and online. They are a big seller whatever venue you choose to purchase from.

Printed in Great Britain
by Amazon